What's in this book

This book belongs to

T0351523

_____

保护动物 Protect the animals

学习内容 Contents

沟通 Communication

认出动物并说说它们
Identify animals and talk about them

生词 New words

★ 它们	they, them
★ 可爱	lovely
★ 身体	body
★ 胖	fat
★ 瘦	thin
★ 因为	because, because of
★ 所以	therefore
★ 牙	tooth
宠物	pet
金鱼	goldfish
斑马	zebra
象	elephant

背景介绍：
学生们准备坐校巴去参观动物保护中心。

句式 Sentence patterns

因为小狗病了，所以它变瘦了。
The dog is getting thinner because it is sick.

因为动物是我们的朋友，所以我们要保护它们。
We have to protect animals because they are our friends.

跨学科学习 Project

地球上濒临绝种的动物
Earth's endangered animals

文化 Cultures

中西文化中龙的象征
The symbolic meanings of
dragons in Chinese and
Western cultures

参考答案：
1 They are going to the Animal Protection Centre.
2 Because they need special care and protection.
3 We should treat them with love and care.

Get ready

1 Where are the students going?

2 Why do you think some pets and animals live there?

3 How do you think we should treat pets and animals?

故事大意：
开车去动物保护中心前，吴老师让学生们说说自己养的宠物，并和大家讨论对动物制品的看法，由此教导学生应该保护动物。

tā men kě ài ma
它们可爱吗？

我们用"它"来指代人以外的单个事物。当不止一个事物时，我们用"它们"。

"你们家里有宠物吗？它们可爱吗？"老师问。

参考问题和答案：

1 Do you think the toy animals Ms Wu is holding are cute? (Yes, they are.)
2 Why did the students raise their hands? (Because Ms Wu asked them a question and they all want to answer it.)

"我有金鱼。它有胖胖的身体、大大的眼睛。"爱莎说。

参考问题和答案：
1 What pet does Elsa keep? (She keeps goldfish.)
2 What do Elsa's goldfish look like? (They have fat and round bodies and big eyes.)

参考问题和答案：
1 Do Hao Hao and Ivan look sad? (Yes, they do.)
2 Why are they sad? (Because Brownie has been sick and therefore lost weight recently. They are worried about Brownie.)

shòu
瘦

yīn wèi
因为

suǒ yǐ
所以

"因为……所以……" 表示一件事的原因和结果，常连用，也可分开单独使用。

"我有小狗。因为它最近病了，所以它变瘦了。"浩浩说。

"牙"是牙齿的通称。吴老师手中图片里的是大象的牙齿，叫"象牙"。

yá

牙

吴老师拿出一些动物制品（斑马皮包、象牙制品）的照片，让大家讨论对其看法。

"这些斑马皮包和象牙盒子，你们会用吗？"老师问。

参考问题和答案：

Ms Wu is holding pictures of some products. What are these products made of? (The bags are made of zebra skin. The box and carvings are made of ivory.)

bān mǎ
斑马

"我不用！我在动物园见过斑马。斑马很可爱！"伊森说。

参考问题和答案：
Do you think Ethan will use the products made of zebra skin? Why or why not? (No, he will not. Because he thinks zebras are cute.)

"因为动物是我们的朋友，所以我们
要保护它们。"伊森说。

Let's think

1 Recall the story. Put a tick or a cross. 提醒学生回忆故事，观察第5至8页。

2 What would you do if you saw a stray or disabled animal on the street? Discuss with your friend.

参考答案：
I would phone the Animal Protection Centre and ask them to help the animals./I would ask my parents for opinions and see if we could help them.

老师应提醒学生，爱护动物的同时也要保护好自己。在路边看到流浪动物时，应尽量避免直接接触，以防被咬伤或被传染疾菌。最好的方法是告诉大人，请大人帮忙想办法救助这些动物

New words

02 1 Learn the new words.

因为　所以　身体　牙　象　斑马　宠物　可爱　胖　金鱼　它们　瘦

2 Listen to your friend and point to the correct words above.

听听说说 Listen and say

第一题录音稿：

1 爱莎有五条可爱的金鱼。

2 因为布朗尼吃了很多饼干所以它变胖了。

3 这个动物园里有斑马，没有羊。

1 Listen and circle the mistakes.

1

2

3

2 Look at the pictures. Listen to the story a

妈妈，因为小动物很可爱，所以我喜欢它们。

因为动物是我们的朋友，所以我们

第二题参考问题和答案：

1 What are Hao Hao, Ling Ling and Mum doing?
(They are looking after animals at the Animal Protection Centre.)

2 Would you like to take care of the animals at the Animal Protection Centre? Why or why not?
(Yes, I want to help the animals./No, because I am allergic to animals.)

第三题延伸活动：

除了题目中的几对反义词外，还可加上已学的，如"上/下""高/矮""冷/热"等。老师随意说出几个，学生说出其相应的反义词，并用动作表示。

 这只小猫很胖，那只小狗很瘦。

 它们很喜欢吃饼干。

护它们。

3 Complete the sentences.
Write the letters and say.

a 多　b 胖　c 瘦　d 前

1

这是小鸟的 _d_ 面和后面。

2

红色小鸟比紫色小鸟 _b_ 。

3

紫色小鸟比红色小鸟 _c_ 。

4

大树上面的小鸟 _a_ 。

Task

Find out which animals
your classmates like.
Write the numbers.

动物	多少人喜欢？	多少人见过？
猫		
狗		
金鱼		
斑马		
大象		
熊猫		
老虎		

Game

Listen to your teacher and point to the correct pets.

艾文的宠物不见了。它是一只胖胖的白色的大狗。它在哪里？
中间最大的白狗

小黄很胖，牙很大。它的耳朵不长。它在哪里？
最左侧露牙的黄狗

Chant

 Listen and say.

我有一只大花猫，

它有白色的毛毛，

身体胖胖像个包。

我有一只大黄狗，

它有黑色的眼睛，

身体胖胖像个球。

我们喜欢猫和狗，

大家都是好朋友。

生活用语 Daily expressions

小心！

Be careful!

不小心。

Careless.

写一写 Write

提醒学生注意这两个字的笔顺。其中"因"外面的国字框和"口"字不一样，国字框的两竖垂直，字形略长；"口"字两竖均向内倾斜。全包围结构的"因"字先写外面上半部分的框，再写里面的部件，最后封口。

1 Trace and write the characters.

丨 冂 冂 冃 冈 因

丶 ソ 为 为

因	为	因	为
因	为	因	为

2 Write and say.

因为 它吃了很多，所以它的身体胖胖的。

因为 它病了，所以它不高兴。

3 Fill in the blanks with the correct words.
Colour in the paws using the same colours.

黄色

蓝色

岁

因为

粉红色 它

从第一句看，缺少了名字叫布朗尼的主体，
故只有"它"适合。其他粉红色横线所在句子
都少了主体，故都可以填入"它"。第二句中，
"三"后面应加"岁"来表示年龄。第三句中，
由关键词"所以"可推出前面应填"因为"。

它 叫布朗尼。 它 今年三 岁
了。 因为 它 很喜欢吃，所以 它
胖胖的。

朋友们喜欢 它 ， 因为 它 很
可爱。我也爱我的宠物。

拼音输入法 Pinyin input

Choose the correct pictures for the
input methods. Write the letters.

Phonetic-based method a

Shape-based method b

There are two methods to write
Chinese on a computer. The phonetic-
based method allows pronunciations
to be converted into characters. The
shape-based method is based on
the structure of the characters.

以读音为基础的输入法，输入声母和韵母会
出现发音相同或相似的字、词。以字形和笔
画为基础的输入法，输入笔画和重要部件即
会出现相关字、词。

a

zhongwen

1 中文
2 中温
3 钟文
4 钟雯

b

中卜大

1 交
2 文
3 放
4 夜
5 效
6 送

多元学习 Connections

Cultures

1 The dragon is an ancient mythical creature in both Eastern and Western cultures. Which dragon do you like?

The Chinese dragon is a symbol of power, strength and good luck for people. It is also the imperial symbol of the Emperors of China.

The Western dragon is a legendary and mythical creature. It is aggressive and warlike. Its blood often contains magical powers.

2 Help the knight find the right dragon head. Circle it.

哪一个头是它的呢？

根据图片，老师可以和学生讨论动物濒危的原因。

1 打猎：合法打猎有利于物种可持续发展。而非法打猎会造成动物濒危，如藏羚羊、观赏鸟类和蛇类等因过度打猎而濒危。

2 自然灾害：龙卷风、水灾和火灾等自然灾害会对动物的栖息地和食物等造成威协。如中国长江流域内的洪灾。

3 污染：人类发展造成大气、水和土壤的污染，影响动物生长与繁衍，栖息地减少。

4 食物链：食物链环环相扣，如人类大量捕食海洋鱼类，造成食物链顶端的海豚、鲸类濒危。

5 迁徙：迁徙中食物和迁徙地不足，以及动物伤亡等情况。

6 干旱：干旱导致水源和粮食短缺，如非洲津巴布韦的大象、野犬等因干旱大量死亡。

Project

1 There are many reasons why there are endangered animals. Learn about them.

Hunting

Natural disaster

Pollution

Food chain

Migration

Drought

2 Match the animals to the correct locations. Discuss with your friend why these animals are endangered.

a 老虎（人类偷猎；栖息地丧失）　b 熊猫（食物来源少；栖息地破坏）　c 大象（资源竞争；人类偷猎）

北极熊（气候变化；食物减少）

因为可爱的动物变少了，所以我们要保护它们。

鲸（气候变化；过度捕杀）

鳄鱼（环境污染；过度捕杀）

海豚（环境污染；过度捕杀）

19

 温习 **Checkpoint**

游戏方法：
学生先完成所有题目，然后将题目中的图片对应拼图，填写题号，完成拼图。

1 Complete the tasks to play the puzzle game.
Write the numbers in the boxes.

① Say 'It is very thin.' in Chinese.

它非常瘦。

② What is the opposite of '瘦'?

胖

9	8	4
1	6	3
7	2	5

③

大象真可爱。

因为动物是我们的朋友，所以我们要保护它们。

④ Why should we protect the animals? Answer in Chinese.

⑥ 它们是什么动物？ Answer in Chinese.

它们是斑马和长颈鹿。

⑨ Write 'because' in Chinese.

⑦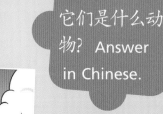

金鱼的身体胖胖的。

⑤ 因为它吃了很多，所以它胖了。

因 为

⑧ Say 'My pet has 16 teeth.' in Chinese.

我的宠物有16颗牙齿。

2 Work with your friend. Colour the stars and the chillies.

Words	说	读	写
它们	☆	☆	🌶
可爱	☆	☆	🌶
身体	☆	☆	🌶
胖	☆	☆	🌶
瘦	☆	☆	🌶
因为	☆	☆	☆
所以	☆	☆	🌶
牙	☆	☆	🌶
宠物	☆	🌶	🌶
金鱼	☆	🌶	🌶

Words and sentences	说	读	写
斑马	☆	🌶	🌶
象	☆	🌶	🌶
因为小狗病了，所以它变瘦了。	☆	🌶	🌶
因为动物是我们的朋友，所以我们要保护它们。	☆	🌶	🌶

Identify animals and talk about them	☆

3 What does your teacher say?

评核建议：

根据学生课堂表现，分别给予"太棒了！(Excellent!)"、"不错！(Good!)"或"继续努力！(Work harder!)"的评价，再让学生圈出左侧对应的表情，以记录自己的学习情况。

My teacher says ...

分享 Sharing

延伸活动：

1 学生用手遮盖英文，读中文单词，并思考单词意思；
2 学生用手遮盖中文单词，看着英文说出对应的中文单词；
3 学生四人一组，尽量运用中文单词分角色复述故事。

Words I remember

它们	tā men	they, them
可爱	kě ài	lovely
身体	shēn tǐ	body
胖	pàng	fat
瘦	shòu	thin
因为	yīn wèi	because, because of
所以	suǒ yǐ	therefore
牙	yá	tooth
宠物	chǒng wù	pet
金鱼	jīn yú	goldfish
斑马	bān mǎ	zebra
象	xiàng	elephant

Other words

问	wèn	to ask
最近	zuì jìn	recently
病	bìng	to fall ill
变	biàn	to become
这些	zhè xiē	these
皮包	pí bāo	leather bag
盒子	hé zi	box
会	huì	to be likely to
用	yòng	to use
过	guò	(auxiliary word of tense)
要	yào	must
保护	bǎo hù	to protect
猫	māo	cat

Oxford University Press is a department of the University of Oxford.
It furthers the University's objective of excellence in research, scholarship,
and education by publishing worldwide. Oxford is a registered trade mark of
Oxford University Press in the UK and in certain other countries

Published in Hong Kong by
Oxford University Press (China) Limited
39th Floor, One Kowloon, 1 Wang Yuen Street, Kowloon Bay,
Hong Kong

Illustrated by Anne Lee, Emily Chan, KK Ng, KY Chan and Wildman

Photographs for reproduction permitted by Dreamstime.com

China National Publications Import & Export (Group) Corporation is an authorized distributor of
Oxford Elementary Chinese.

Please contact content@cnpiec.com.cn or 86-10-65856782

ISBN: 978-0-19-942994-3

10 9 8 7 6 5 4 3 2

Teacher's Edition
ISBN: 978-0-19-082259-0

10 9 8 7 6 5 4 3 2